Develop Your Emotional Armor

By

Shawn P. West, MEng, MBB

Publication Details

About the Author

As a decorated combat veteran and an accomplished Aerospace Engineer in which Shawn earned his Master's Degree, he has passion for education, personal growth and mentoring. Through experience and observations, he expanded his field of knowledge on the more important issues facing society today—verbal and emotional abuse. Everyone deserves to be successful, yet there are many who are challenged with overt degradation and emotional pain caused by resentment or other upsetting life events. These negative experiences lead to low self-esteem which can reduce the quality of a person's life in many forms.

The inspiration behind this book, "*Develop Your Emotional Armor*," was built upon a retrospective view of those who were bullied and taken advantage of as well as those who experienced a significant emotional life event. Over the years, Shawn witnessed the prevalence of negative influences and how they affect almost every aspect of our lives, from how we think about ourselves to the way we think about or react to life situations. Seeing those who felt traumatized, insecure and socially isolated has encouraged him to intervene on their behalf. He laid the foundation for the emotional armor with his assertion that improving an individual's self-confidence could not only lead them to success but also help them become resilient and overcome societies negativity.

Develop Your Emotional Armor is about a person's ability to mount a layer of defense or a psychological coping mechanism for self-protection against verbal abuse. In this book, Shawn outlines the steps and developmental processes to enhance one's self-worth. He provides practical approaches to address and reduce the impact of PTSD, bullying, verbal aggressions, and insults. He finds it important for every person to equip themselves with this armor, making them less vulnerable to negative verbal attacks.

He argues that the reason people are affected with bullying is not solely because of their appearance, capability, sexuality or gender but their attitude towards it.

Shawn wrote this book to inspire the readers to believe in themselves and to not let negativity dictate who they really are. He looks forward to educating more people by sharing his knowledge about emotional armor and helping them build lasting confidence that will change the way they think about themselves.

Dedication

This book is affectionately dedicated to my inspiration and life coach, thank you for teaching me priceless life lessons and sharing wisdom with daily conversation. We truly share unconditional love.

– My Mother, Roberta.

And my Father Al (Plato), for your unwavering dedication to provide, and instilling, timeless country truisms that inspire and motivate me.

Acknowledgment

Over the years I've been blessed to have had exposure and be influenced my amazing spiritual brothers and sisters, work colleagues and some of the finest scholars in the world.

My body of work within the need to "Develop Your Emotional Armor" is about focusing on an awareness and the need to cultivate a personal internal coping mechanism that protects feelings that drive emotions.

The topics discussed are timely and important. It pulls together relevant situations that can cause a significant emotional event. This is not an ordinary book. The well thought out and informed practices presented within the pages to follow will help you recognize and take control of your situation and realize the emotional balance you want and need.

Develop Your Emotional Armor is it an expression of provocative reflection on real life events and scenarios that I want to shed light in order to help all ages, gender and ethnicities.

Special thanks those for contributing to the inperation behind my wiriting: Roberta Edwards, Alfred Edwards, Krystal D. West, Ray Raigosa, Marc Alain Amio, Tyler Granholm, Dean Granholm, Gina Inofinada, Greg Graves, Nicholas C. Amodeo, Drew Aliperto, and Ibn Edwards.

Table of Contents

Publication Details iii

About the Author iv

Dedication..vii

Acknowledgment...viii

Preface xii

Chapter 1...1

Chapter 2...24

Chapter 3...40

Chapter 4...55

Chapter 5...73

Chapter 6...90

Chapter 7...108

Page Blank Intentionally

Preface

There is an interesting psychological coping mechanism that all humans have when dealing with certain emotional interactions, particularly criticisms and uncomfortable conversations that pierce our confidence and sway our self-esteem. Some people do their best to keep their emotions at bay by concealing their emotional selves and reacting more appropriately. This psychological coping mechanism and controlled emotional sharing is often due to a form of self-protection called *emotional armor*.

The easiest way to picture this tangible psychological coping mechanism is to imagine an impenetrable plating like titanium steel under a person's skin, or similar to the exterior suits of armor worn by knights when going into battle in the past. The purpose of those extra layers of steel was twofold. First, from a psychological viewpoint, the suit provided peace of mind and a level of confidence to the fighter by alleviating the fear of being vulnerable or exposed during the battle. Second, from a physical viewpoint, it provided a real concrete protection against the enemy's attacks by interfering with their ability to land any critical or life-ending blows. These two factors play a similar psychological role in our modern-day use of emotional armor.

Every human being experiences a criticism at some point in their lives. Negative comments can be received differently by people and can have a detrimental effect on a person's wellbeing. Some individuals respond to criticism in a less emotional and more cerebral manner. They develop their emotional armor and use some techniques to cope with the situation in a more intelligent and appropriate manner.

There are two layers of emotional armor. The first layer protects ourselves against degradation, abuse, insult, and being constantly upset. The inner layer helps us build lasting self-confidence to control our emotions and react more appropriately. This book outlines the important ingredients and recipes needed to develop your own emotional armor.

Chapter 1

Has This Happened to You?

It is fair to say that in a lifetime we all are exposed to a significant emotional event that could alter the course of our lives. It could be a real world situation that appears on the television or a personal experience that causes us to examine our own coping mechanism to continue a balanced approach to life. In my experience, there have been many situations where the emotional scales of balance were tested. Let me share a real life event illustrating the need to develop emotional armor.

It was May 3rd, 2011 when I first came to terms with the fact that my life would not be the same anymore. Bin Laden was dead and the youth of America seemed elated. From a grubby plywood building at a small rural outpost in

Afghanistan, a gentle sense of jealousy ran through me as CNN beamed images of my millennial peers celebrating and chanting 'U-S-A!' at their campuses, and high-fiving at the dual benefits of the demise of our childhood boogeyman and the blissful naïveté that the Global War on Terrorism was possibly over.

I, however, was nearing the end of my first career deployment. It just did not feel fair to me. In that moment, I wanted so badly to feel the same relief they felt. I wished I could be there with them. I ached for the opportunity to forget where I was, and to just be 21 years old with them. Instead, I chose yet another target: 'Objective BROKEN ARROW.'

I remember that mission clearly, the chilly Afghan air at dawn, and how strange it felt to walk through the empty and dusty streets of a sleepy village while we closed in on the target. After a few minutes of adjustment and refinement, my equipment finally showed that we were within just 100 yards of the target ... until the battery powering my directional antenna suddenly died. My gear's failure felt like a tragicomical metaphor for my beleaguered psyche. I fished around my backpack to grab a spare and realized that I had left it on the charger in haste. We had struck out and BROKEN ARROW got away. Three weeks and a handful of missions later, I spent my 22nd birthday in Kandahar, more disconnected from home than ever – a feeling I blamed on the responsibilities that I had volunteered as a soldier.

Since then, I have grappled with what exactly it means to be a veteran. Today, I am still not comfortable or confident with assigning a one-size-fits-all description of what constitutes our experience. While more trivial and vastly overplayed tropes of vets (increased personal discipline or unsettling combat nightmares, for example) certainly hold true for me, and are likely to be true for many veterans, these exist the side effects of change, rather than the change itself.

Society, whether through some sort of corporate adoration gimmick or via skewed depictions of combat veterans as an emotionally unstable collective in the media, usually misunderstands and paints characterizations of the veteran experience that lack meaningful depth. So instead, I am choosing to highlight, in detail, just one facet when I noticed a considerable change in myself – a marked difference in how I approach responsibility.

As soon as I enlisted in the military, the forces of the government were hard at work redefining my own understanding of responsibility. 'HOLD this over your head! CLEAN the dirt off this rock! SPEAK in this way! WHY does this rock not have dirt on it?' My drill sergeants would scream day in and day out. Ridiculous commands and questions would come for hours until a soldier finally lapsed, which always led to the platoon being punished en masse.

The lapse of the individual was now the failure of the group. Daily, this message was constantly reinforced to new recruits by rotating us through endless mental and physical exercises that were undoubtedly designed for us to fail. Uncle Sam knew that failure was the best instructor. One realized quickly that the defect of a teammate or the poor decision of a single leader could result in a situation where everyone loses. This instilled a dire need to avoid being that person at all costs – a process which may have begun out of simple self-interest but nearly always transformed into genuine brotherhood. It was something fueled by unwillingness to cause harm to your brother in arms.

Through this, the army teaches that your responsibilities change the lives of those around you. When one fails to act, others also fail because of it. As my career progressed, my responsibilities grew larger. I moved from being simulated to real-world situations, and from small stakes to greater ones. Within a few years I worked myself into a career littered with posts where I would have responsibilities with international impacts.

It was in this kind of position that I later found myself during my third and final trip to Afghanistan. It had been almost four years since my first rotation. I was hard at work with the National Mission Force – the special operation that hunts down the most wanted terrorists for the U.S. Our headquarters looked like something out of a Hollywood movie. The whole place was covered with oversized video screens, each displaying a different operational video feed from various aerial sources. For each feed, several statistics were shown, such as the drone type and altitude as well as big yellow lettering across the top indicating which target was being monitored.

One morning, on the way to my desk, something unusual caught my eye. There, in big lettering, on the target boards, was the word 'BROKEN ARROW.' My heart skipped a beat. Immediately, I asked a friend what he knew about the target, as I started to mentally convince myself that it must have been a simple duplicate name.

That happens quite frequently, I thought. Plus, it did not make sense that my BROKEN ARROW – a low level thug – would be a target of national interest. My colleague began describing about it. As his words fell out, my mind faded to blankness as I started to recognize the grainy outline of the same street I had walked on years before. "And in 2013? He took down a Blackhawk, 8 US KIA… not to mention the guys we lost on the recovery missions right after." The words hit me like a freight train and the reality rushed back. An indescribable, awful emotion came over me, and my stomach immediately turned to knots. I excused myself and went back to my room, not even making it halfway before breaking down to weep.

Deep down I knew that I was, at the very least, partially responsible for this horrific outcome. What if I had simply remembered to bring that battery? What if I had located him faster with my gear? What if he was the middle-aged Afghani we ran into when we exfiltrated? Why did we not come back for him? For weeks, the hypotheticals never ended in my head. When I could not sleep, all the time, I put in additional hours acting out of a fevered madness that would make Ahab proud, and wanting to atone for my failure. It was all in vain with BROKEN ARROW eventually vanishing to the haven of Pakistan.

Sadly, I have many stories like this one. Resulting from far-reaching responsibilities tied to work, my greatest successes and accomplishments have been lauded both privately and in the press but I know from experience that the failures come with an equally monumental burden. I can personally attest to the fact that these failures in responsibility, innocent as they may have been at the time, indeed resulted in the loss of my brothers. I know first-hand how much this hurts and how much it forces you to grow and adapt to constantly refine and improve yourself, all to insure that it does not happen again on watch.

When suffering from emotional complications, there is no 'right' or 'wrong' way to feel, think, or respond to a situation. Hence, a person going through these complications should not pressurize themselves by comparing their own reaction to someone else who is going through a similar situation. Just remember that their responses are normal reactions and when something really extraordinary happens to you, then your actions toward those events are understandable. As long as the actions of the sufferer are not hurting someone, or are not breaking the law, all your actions are right.] *But are they?*

People around the ones who are suffering also need to understand that sometimes even they cannot help the person going through psychological pain, it is not necessary that their words and actions will miraculously heal someone. So, there is no way of knowing what to do unless you get the advice of a professional in the industry.

The methods which are used to recognize psychological and emotional trauma have improved drastically in the recent era. In fact, they have undergone a revolution throughout the years within the other half of the 20th century. Before this breakthrough, the psychologists would only keep those men under observation who had been through catastrophic wars. According to them, they were the only ones who had suffered through psychological trauma.

The women's movement, which took place in the 1960s, broadened the horizons of the doctors. This brought to life the violence and sexual abuse against women and children. Therefore, they were included in the list of people who suffered traumatic events and were affected mentally by it. As the years progressed and studies further expanded, a lot of aspects were learned about trauma in the 1990s. This furthered the research about the psychological aspects of pain and the definition of traumatic events has even progressed even more.

The Signs and Symptoms

In addition to the doctors learning more about the brain through psychological tests, there are more methods available to the doctors now. MRI and CT scans of the brain have granted more exposure to the mental conditions of a human. With these tests, researches and doctors alike are now able to observe the brain as it reacts to things. These brain scans have helped bring to life the fact that a trauma has the potential to change the structure and the function of the brain.

However, not everyone needs a CT or an MRI to suspect that a person is going through something mentally challenging. There are many probable signs that can let a person know whether they themselves or someone they know is suffering from a psychological trauma. One of the most prominent signs that anyone can see in a person is that the sufferer can appear shaken and disoriented at times. This is most prominent when they are unable to respond to conversation as they normally do. Instead, they may often appear withdrawn or lost even when they are talking to someone.

Another sign of a person going through psychological trauma is anxiety. Anxiety due to trauma can take refuge in multiple things which can include irritability, night terrors, poor concentration, edginess, and mood swings. Although these symptoms of trauma are quite mainstream, they are not the only things that can be used for conclusive evidence of an emotional trauma. It all depends upon the behavior of the individual going through this ordeal. This is the reason why trauma can be unnoticeable even to the sufferer's closest friends and family.

Cases like these highlight the importance of talking to someone after a highly life-changing event has occurred in a person's life. Even if a person shows no signs of being disturbed mentally, there is a possibility that some psychological change has occurred. Trauma can actually take over the person's mind for days, months, or even years after the actual event has occurred.

When the person is suffering from the emotional trauma, it can be hard for them to accept that they indeed are a victim of psychological disturbance. Along with coping with the trauma, the person can go through denial, sadness,

not necessarily

emotional outbursts, or anger. The person going through the trauma may direct their emotions toward other people. These people are of course the ones who are closest to the victim.

They could be either friends or family members, roommates or coworkers. The victim lashing out at all the other people around them is due to the reason that the condition could be really bad. It is difficult to help a person who is pushing all the people around them away from them. However, with thorough understanding of the emotional symptoms that have developed after a traumatic event, the pain can be eased. : Pain can't be cased by another person i can only show understanding + care.

Another form of discovering an emotional struggle can be with the physical signs that their body is displaying. These physical signs may include the paleness of the skin, feeling lethargic, having fatigue all the time, poor concentration, or an increased heartrate. The victim of the emotional trauma may have anxiety or panic attacks. Due to this, the person may be unable to cope in certain situations that demand presence of mind or skills. The physical symptoms that occur due to emotional struggle can be just as damaging and evident as the ones suffered in a physical injury. These physical signs need the same amount of care as required in bodily damages. Just because someone shows less symptoms than expected does not mean that they do not deserve care required to treat a patient. ⟋

Timing of the Trauma

As mentioned earlier, emotional trauma does not simply happen on a specific time. It could be in development for years within your system or it can take over you within the length of a day. This all depends upon the things that you have suffered through. Perhaps all your life you were abused physically by a parent. Perhaps you were not able to defend yourself when one of your parents or your sibling was hitting you repeatedly. At that moment, you did not react to anything and took the pace of your life as it was. The abuse could have stopped and you finally forgot everything.] Many abuse victims don't forget.

However, many years later, you encounter a situation when someone you know hits you and you still do not have the chance to defend yourself. This experience can trigger the memories from your childhood and you may learn that you are still at a weak spot. It can have you look in the past how you grew with being hit on physically. All the feelings that have been building up ever since your childhood, that you had kept at bay until now are out in the open now. These feelings are now consuming you and are a hindrance to the way you think, act, and talk. They have made you emotionally unstable and you are hurting from the inside.

In another scenario, the trauma could take into effect due to a sudden event that just occurred with you. You may have witnessed something that shook you to the very core and you cannot get over the situation that had transpired in front of your eyes. This situation could be a fatal accident that happened in front of you or it could be a bad accident that happened to you while you were driving. There are plenty of things that could make you go in shock and give you something that you would remember for your lifetime. But for now, you have become damaged emotionally.

Something that you never thought happens to you or in front of you. This could be a rough way of seeing death so close to you. It can trigger all the negative emotions within you. It can make you think that there was something that you could do to stop all of it from happening. Even though you did everything you could, or there was nothing that was in your control, the emotional trauma can still persist.

Many times, the emotional suffering can start all of a sudden with the initial shock of what you just witnessed or what just happened to you. The person may need to be escorted as they may even freeze in their place from the initial shock. On the other hand, they can simply walk on their own and then contemplate the events that have happened with them. Short-term and long-term effects of trauma may be very much like each other but long-term effects are more severe than short-term ones. Short-term mood changes are considered normal behavior when a person is suffering from a trauma. But if the shifts in mood last for longer than a few weeks, a long-term effect can take place which will result in traumatic psychological disorders. → CHECK?

Conditions of a Traumatic Experience

There would be times when you may start wondering whether you are suffering from a psychological trauma or simply having a mood swing. Although mood swings could be of different lengths yet they are not going to be as long-lasting as an emotional trauma. You may feel irritated by something or you may feel bad about an event that happened to you but that is a natural reaction. This does not mean that you are emotionally unstable or have an everlasting depression. Instead, it is something that you will recover from within a few hours or within a few days. [However, depression is something that you are not able to simply 'bounce back' from. It takes time.] **medication?**

There are people who have been battling depression for quite a long time and they are not succeeding in their battle. Some people recover quickly from the emotional pain that they are suffering from and do not let the terrible things that happened to them be of any value in their future life. However, a person who is going through emotional trauma is not able to think straight for a prolonged period of time and is incapable of making a decision without being guided in the simplest of task. They can be considered depressed.

For these people, the memories of the recent work that they did become foggy and they are not able to do tasks that they once performed easily. They become disconnected from the things that they are doing presently and they are not able to do anything that is new to them. Instead, they find ways to dodge a situation so that they would have to do no work at all. *Depression is not necessarily from trauma.*

This dodging of situations could be the reason why most people who are suffering from emotional trauma can appear lethargic or lazy. When often told to do something, they

Most people tend to procastinate?

simply procrastinate that task until it is too late for them to do. They may also lay off that task and do it haphazardly at the end. Things for these people are at the extreme end. They are not exactly in the right frame of mind when they are doing something and can even have trouble in executing a perfectly defined plan.

In another case, the way you can judge whether or not you are emotionally unwell is when your emotional responses to even the simplest of situation and conversation are at the extreme ends. Although there are many people who may have temperament that enables them to take rash decision. But while suffering emotionally this attitude can take birth in a mentally traumatized person. You can take an example of a situation when your brain decides that there is 'danger' around, it triggers the primal 'fight or flight' response.

This may not be the most reasonable response but is the most convenient option that you brain has come up with. Why is that so? This is because you have a lot of things going on. You are thinking about the things that happened to you which have put you in emotional turmoil. This is why your brain cannot process the new information that you have just discovered. Instead of revaluating your decisions, you are simply going to go ahead with the plan.

Sleep is also the primary response that you can see being affected by the emotional struggle that your body is going through. Insomnia is a common condition in the people with emotional trauma. Even if you are getting more sleep than usual, you may still end up feeling tired. You suffer from a disturbed sleep which may wake you up at unexpected time in the middle of the night.

18

Your dream patterns may change and you may have more confusing dreams than ever. In fact, it is common to develop night panic attacks while suffering from emotional battles. In these panic attacks, you can suddenly wake up with a heartrate that is more than normal. You may also end up feeling severe anxiety after you wake up.

When your mind is stressed and is trying to make sense of a situation that is difficult, it does not leave much room for you to deal with other matters that require your attention. You may be required to present something in a meeting but you are incapable of even reading through the presentation because you have a lot of things going on in your mind that are important to you. There are multiple ways that this defect in your attention can occur.

You may also be listening to someone speaking with you but you are not able to grasp truly what they are saying to you. This is because in this situation your mind is still occupied with a lot that has affected you emotionally. Even though you are trying your best to communicate and have a healthy conversation, you are simply incapable of doing so.

→ memories & emotions don't go away; you learn to cope w/ it.
Have / Becomes a new norm

Being emotionally damaged means you are simply living with the memories and emotions of the past. You are not making new memories, and the ones that you do create are simply going to be complex emotions. Hence, your brain simply brings out all the past mistakes that you did or the terrible things that happened to you. Since you are already feeling bad, you will end up feeling even worse. There will often be times when you feel like there has been nothing going right in your life and you have never had a moment in your lifetime that you could be proud of. You always stress yourself and you are able to replay all the accomplishments that you have made.

unable 2 otherwise its contradicting.

There are times when you feel stronger and you encounter thoughts such as "I am bigger than this and I can counter this situation easily." You may yourself feel like the victim and may want to step out of that by saying to yourself, "I am not going to let this happen to me again." In both these scenarios, the person going through the emotional trauma is suffering and they know this to be a fact. However, they are making every effort that they can on their own to get out of that mentality. They are trying to leave behind the thoughts that bring them down.

A person who goes into an emotional trauma often shocks the people around them when they start reacting to simple situations with emotions that are not expected of them. They change their perspective on things. Their perspective on ordinary occurrences also varies from their previous opinions. Furthermore, a person who is usually social may end up avoiding company of the people. They may want to be completely alone and not talk to anyone. This may happen when the person does not want anyone to know what their feelings are. They want to be isolated so that they can deal with their problems alone.

On the contrary, a person may also completely change their behavior and could be very outgoing while they really liked to stay alone before the trauma occurred with them. This could happen when the person is trying to occupy their mind with something else. This could also manifest as unusual behavior as this is not your personality and you are not used to reacting this way. This may come across as

Do people always change their behavior in the opposite manner?

somewhat of an improvement of yourself and your attitude, but most often it is defense mechanism for your emotions.

With all these aspects combined you may be suffering from a traumatic emotional experience. You may be able to escape from all of these complex emotions in different ways that will be elaborated in this book. The process may be long and hard but with the will to change yourself, you can overcome that emotional struggle by taking control of your life. You will not just eliminate the emotional trauma but you will very well build a defense mechanism that will protect you from further emotional imbalances as well.

Questions to Ask Yourself ?

Q. Is it possible for everyone to get over the trauma despite how severe it was?

Ans. Indeed it is possible for everyone. There may be some tragic incidents that may push the person into deep isolation but the person can surely get over it with the passage of time.

Q. With whose help you would be able to get over the trauma?

Ans. Anyone worthy of trust.

↓
professional

Q. How long it would take to get over the trauma?

Ans. As we have all heard that good things do not come easy, similarly getting over a trauma is not easy as well. It is more likely to take time but it will be worth it. The perception about life will be changed.

① Story is the beginning.
② Memories & emotions don't necessarily go away, one learns to cope with it, developing a new norm.
③ Mentioning medical/professional advice
④ Questions to ask yourself section: different title? thought it was list of questions to determine if you're struggling w/ trauma

⑤ Pg 20: Able to unable .

23

Chapter 2

Foundational Building of the Emotional Armor

Children are the most vulnerable beings amongst all. They mold their thoughts the way they are taught by their elders or how they see people doing around them. Any child who looks at their father doing household chores, like cleaning the dishes or throwing the trash out, adapts to this habit when they grow older. Similarly, when a child looks at their mother working hard for her family and getting a job, the kids register this action as something good.

Initial stages of trying to build an emotional armor include maturity, responsibility, and other aspects such as being persistent.

Most parents believe in giving their children the best of everything. They try and provide them with the best schooling possible within their budget. They want their kids to eat the best healthy food so that they maintain a good health. Furthermore, they want their kids to have a comfortable bedroom, a good lifestyle, and every gadget that will help their kids progress in life or keep them entertained. However, despite these things, kids can grow up to be mentally disturbed. This is because they do not get the attention, the love, and the care that the parents are supposed to give them.

Of course, parents want the best of everything for their children but they forget that despite all the luxuries that they provide their children with, the child still craves their presence and attention the most. They like you to be present there when they do something extraordinary in their life. Something that may look ordinary to us, like coloring while staying within the lines, is somewhat of an achievement for a little child. They want to celebrate it by showing it to their parents and get their appreciation on accomplishing such a feat. However, what about the

→ nature vs nurture

children who grow up with both parents around them yet are disturbed?)

In some cases, the parents are even present in front of the children when they need them. They are there to celebrate every little achievement that their child makes and console them when something terrible happens. Yet, the tensions within the parents' lives can reflect on their child. Just like they see that you love them and care for them, they also observe your behavior toward other people around you.

Your life partner, your other children, and even your relatives and friends who come to visit you are under your child's radar. As evident by the behavior of many children in our lives, the adults are responsible for helping the children learn new things. Grown-ups are the guiding tools for these developing minds. The kids look at the day-to-day conversations of everyone around them and converse in a similar manner. Adult helps children to think about why and how things happen. w/ Globalization + social media : more teachers

Seeing new things helps them understand how to live their own life. So why are these children engulfed by depression? When they see strained relationship around

26

them or see people fighting with each other, it is going to affect their thought process. When their thought process gets deeply affected by these disturbances, they get stressed.

They simply want to shut out the bad things that happen to them and want to simply look at the positive side of life. When a person is emotionally damaged, they will act very similar to that child who has an increased stress level due to the complexities they face in life. They will try to escape from anything that challenges them emotionally only due to the fear of not getting depressed. Instead, they appear to be cold and uncaring about the feelings of others. This condition that they are displaying can be termed emotional armor.

Emotionally damaged act similar to kid?

Emotional Armor = cold & uncaring about feelings of others.

This emotional armor blocks out all the people from their life who hurt them emotionally. They form this barrier to save themselves from getting depressed, or having a stressed thought process. The blockage of emotions can be directed at specific people or everyone and everything around them. They are in constant fear that someone is going to hurt them emotionally. It does not matter whether

27

the person is a child or an adult, they are going to display the same response of cutting themselves off from people when it comes to talking about their feelings.

There are two types of emotional armor I want to briefly touch on today. A healthy type of emotional armor is primarily situational. We implement such an emotional armor to protect ourselves against being used, taken advantage of, or being constantly upset. For example, take a physician who is frequently confronted with having to deliver devastating health news. For them to do the job efficiently they must disconnect from their emotional self temporarily in order to be effective, hold themselves together, and manage the horrific situations they regularly encounter. Now this physician is fearless when it comes to suppressing their emotions for their patients.

Many people exhibit an unhealthy type of emotional armor. For example, take the people who we describe as emotionally unavailable because of their inability or unwillingness to connect or interact with others. Their lack of coordination with you and the fact that they do not talk to you about how they are actually feeling about something is not just stressful for them, but a point of worry for you too.

It often takes therapy to break through these defenses because it requires time, trust, patience, love, and understanding to chip away at this armor.

Another example is found in the people whose emotional armor is so easily penetrated that they are constantly getting upset over almost everything that happens in the world, even when it does not directly involve them.

In contrast to the situational protective armor used by the physician, this armor operates more like a sieve and, as a result, they are always vulnerable. It is said that the suits of armor weigh from as little as 45 pounds to more than 100 pounds. By the time the warriors cross the field to engage in battle, they are exhausted carrying this incredible weight.

Similarly, emotional armor can also weigh you down. To anyone who has ever been in a relationship with someone who is emotionally unavailable, you already know the strength of that armor plating. As hard as you try to penetrate it, you are almost always left feeling unappreciated, unheard, ineffective, and unloved. This type of emotional armor creates a wall that keeps people out and, as a result, helps the wearer avoid being emotionally vulnerable and intimate.

To some degree, we all have our own suit of emotional armor. People who build the emotional barrier around them do so because they feel that they cannot afford to be emotionally exposed. [To them, emotional exposure means vulnerability and weakness of yourself.] *not necessarily weakness*

These feelings are common when you have fears about the person that they may hurt you once you are weak, or when you deem that the person is untrustworthy. There are also the people who have developed their emotional armor and find it hard to share their their feelings even with the person they are closest to. They cannot bear to burden themselves with the thoughts related to feelings. It exhausts them and instead of them relieving their problems by discussing it with someone, they feel that they cannot communicate with anyone. This entire bottling-up of emotions can stress anyone, no matter how good emotional barrier they have built for themselves and no matter how long they have been doing it. In fact, the longer they tend to keep their feelings to themselves, the more stressed they would be.

They feel like the other person would not be able to understand their emotional journey and would simply be wasting their time and energy in trying to explain things to someone.

Despite the disadvantages of not being emotionally present sometimes, there are going to be many advantages as well for a person who has developed an emotional armor. This mental toughness can let you become stronger mentally and grant you a sound mind even in the face of adversity. It can protect you from suffering too much when you receive a news that would mentally drain or challenge the person who does not have emotional armor.

When you talk about emotional armor, you are not simply talking about keeping your emotions to yourself all the time, but it also means that you will be in a better position to handle any challenge that demands good presence of mind from you. Not only that, but you would also be able to defend the people around you in a much better way. You

[handwritten margin notes:] Bottling up emotions can have advantage? I understand authors point however it is right after showcasing severe negative effects of emotional armor

[handwritten inline note:] why should you challenge?

31

would be in a better position to take care of them when they are faced with any mentally devastating situation.

When the base of your emotional armor has been strong, it becomes easier for you to be focused and determined. This armor can keep you from deviating and let you be on the right track. The stronger your emotional armor is, the better focused you would be in whatever you do. You would not ponder over what has happened and how it has hurt you, or what could happen and how you must protect yourself from it. All of this would not be a matter of deep concern for you and you can move past all these worries without being too troubled. *Emotional Intelligence: ponder on what happened*

Every person's life is unpredictable, no matter how well they plan it. You do not plan on getting sick or someone close to you passing away. However, these are a part and parcel of life and these things are most often unexpected. In rare circumstances, when you know that you are going to face some form of emotional struggle, preparation is never enough to let you contain your emotions when you finally face the situation. This is because these people do not have an emotional barrier helping them cope up with a situation.

But it just stated preparation is never enough?

32

Nothing that they do would help them keep their emotions from dwindling. This is the time when these people would need the most emotional support from people who have developed the emotional armor.

Isn't it normal to display emotions in time of unexpected situation.

Building your emotional armor starts when you are in an adversary, and you are telling yourself that you will not give up yet continue moving forward. You stop reflecting on the mistakes that happened in the past and turn over a new leaf. When the voice inside your head keeps telling you that you can do something, you will be more inclined to leave every irrelevant work and focus on overcoming that one specific hurdle.

Good to Reflect? Learn from them?

One thing that can help you with building resilience is that you need to manage your expectations accordingly. As you just read, when you are expecting something to happen, you may be prepared to face that situation in a somewhat better way than someone who never expected that thing to occur at all. You may still suffer emotionally but the emotional pain may be less.

In order to complete your emotional armor, you are simply going to be more focused on what your expectations are. If

33

your expectations are poorly managed, then you are simply going to be more vulnerable emotionally and would not be prepared for something more sinister. You will face more surprises and may feel that you are not in control of your life anymore.

Since you are suffering from lack of control over anything, this may weaken your morale and mental fortitude. Having the ability to predict what would happen in your life is a vital component of having a substantial base for your emotional armor. The people who are ready for any kind of possibility are the ones who remain strongly armed and are a lot better at defending themselves.

The more you have the 'go with the flow' kind of attitude, the better chances you have of having things slipping from your hand. One unplanned thing will simply lead to another unplanned thing and the situation will simply roll out the way you never even expected it to be. The best way to deal with such problems is by taking your time and planning the things. When you are planning things, take into consideration the events that can go wrong in that plan. If you do not consider those problems, then you are simply letting your emotional barrier down.

In situations when everything that is happening to you goes out of control, you can still save and adjust your attitude. *"But how can I do that?"* You may ask yourself that question. This can be dealt with reacting to a problem in a certain way. The best way to adjust to a problematic situation is by accepting that it happened, learning from that mistake, and then moving on. The more you ponder over something that happened, the more you would be stuck in the past, and would not be able to focus on the present.

This does not meant that you completely disregard the problem and do not even try to find a solution for it. It simply means that you solve the problem and do not ponder over it for so long that it affects your present. The more you are engrossed in your previous problems, the less time you will have for things going on around you at the present moment.

When you let the emotions get the best of you, you simply are letting them be your driving force. Following the heart may not be your best possible way of living your life. You need to think logically and people who want to build up their own emotional armor just do that. You simply need to listen to the most logical reasoning that your brain is coming up with and then step out of your comfort zone to do it. ↳ **Brain + heart [Emotional Intelligence]**

All of these things lay the basis of building your emotional armor and let you be more resilient in the decisions of your life. When you have finally set these emotions in place, you are on the way to build a better emotional armor for yourself.

what things?

Questions to Ask Yourself

Q. Is it suitable to seek help in developing your emotional armor?

Ans. Consulting a suitable person is advisable to develop a strong emotional armor to help withstand emotional attacks from other people.

Q. Is it necessary to help the young generation with building the armor?

Ans. Yes, helping the young generation with the foundations of the emotional armor will decrease the risk of having them suffer from emotional breakdowns and similar problems.

Q. How to strengthen your emotional armor?

Ans. Constantly check for any weak points within your armor. You may be able to tackle with insults but criticism might have an impact on you. Improvise your weak points and make them your strength.

Q. Can emotional armor affect a person's social life in any way?

Ans. It is not certain that the emotional armor can have a vast impact on an individual's social life, yet it can restrain the person from communicating with new people or maintaining previously established contacts.

Q. What are the negative effects of emotional armor on relationship with your partner?

Wait what?

Ans. It is debatable to some extent that emotional armor can have negative effects on your relationship with your partner as you will be no longer showing signs of attachment and you insecure toward your problems and concerns. This may give spark to unintended conflicts and arguments.

Chapter 3

Dealing with Criticism

As you have learned in the previous chapter, there are many advantages of having an emotional armor, on top of all, it gives you stability and structure in life. It does not let you ponder over simply one thing, instead it lets you move on in life aiming to achieve your true vision. People who have their emotions put together well are those who actually know how to deal with situations the right way. Hearing negative comments from people around you is more likely to convince you of thinking negative about yourself. However, these people are able to survive in a slightly better way than those who are emotionally vulnerable.

People who do not display their emotions at the drop of a hat can survive in tougher environments. They know how to act and what to say. They are usually calm in a situation when any emotional person panics.

An emotional person's feelings are a lot more intense and the effect of those feelings lasts a lot longer than the person who has developed emotional armor. The more the person is emotional, the more difficult it is to get over something that is emotionally traumatizing. It would be harder for them to forget that something bad has happened and to recover from it. When they encounter a situation that can emotionally damage someone, they tend to ponder over the fact of what they could have done to avoid this situation. While looking at your mistakes and learning from them is a good thing, sticking to the past can simply ruin your present.

The whole point of learning with experience is to make mistakes and learn from those mistakes what to do and what not to do, but then move on to something else. An emotionally vulnerable person, however, is not able to do that so easily. They simply evaluate the mistake from all corners, and instead of moving forward after gaining that experience, they simply ponder over it. A situation like this always hinders the present circumstances and the things that require immediate attention simply take a back seat. Later, the things of the present that demand attention become the past and pose an even bigger concern for the worrisome fellow. The chain then continues until the emotionally vulnerable person realizes that they need to stop living in the past and focus on the present.

These types of attitudes are not only present in a professional environment, but also in our personal lives. When a person does a mistake in any relationship, either with their life partner, their immediate or extended family, or even their friends, they are required to accept that mistake, apologize for it, and then move on. However, the case can become critical if the emotionally vulnerable person simply cannot get over the fact that they have done a mistake.

Sometimes, the other party is unforgiving and does not want to do anything with the person who committed the mistake. This prompts the emotionally vulnerable person to constantly try to improve the relationship with the offended person. Things like this then affect their present relationship and have the potential to leave them isolated.

One of the biggest reasons for hovering too much around one mistake is criticism. People who are emotionally stable and who are able to hone their emotional armor, in situations when they are criticized are those who live a happier life. In order to understand how they do this, you need to realize what kind of criticism you are actually facing.

For a long time, the word 'criticize' has been associated with something dreadful. Anyone who criticizes someone is simply hated by the person being criticized. However, that is not always the case in criticism.

It is highly possible that the person who is criticizing you is doing this to bring you down, to point out your flaws, or to bring your morale down. However, there is a chance that the critic is simply trying to make you a better person. They are merely pointing out your flaw so that you can fix it and make an improvement to yourself. Of course, you need to be confident in yourself and in what you do but there is no reason why you should not strive yourself to become better.

If someone is giving you information that can work in your benefit and can let you be an upgraded version of yourself, then do not shut that information out, rather accept it. The more easily you accept that positive criticism, the better your chances are of enhancing yourself. If you try and fight that criticism, then no one stands to lose anything other than you.

This is not to say that you let any type of criticism get to your head. there are a few things that you simply cannot change or do not want to change because they are your individual qualities. For example, you may be better at driving an ordinary car than a sports car. Since you may never need to drive a sports car, and you have no ambition of competing in a race, then someone's criticism on your lack of knowledge in driving a sports car is unhelpful. It does nothing to help you achieve something in life, which is why it is an irrelevant comment for you.

Any criticism that is meant to point a flaw that in no way hinders your life is simply useless. This is the type of criticism you need to keep away from in order to lead a happier life that is devoid of any negative thoughts. The more the person displays emotions even at the slightest of criticism, the bigger chance it gives the people around them to hurt their feelings even more.

Criticizing someone can give some people a false sense of power over those they criticize. It makes those critics feel better about themselves when they hold you in comparison with themselves. Those critics are certainly not the best at everything either. They have their own flaws. These flaws may be different from the ones you have but there are flaws in everyone. Just because you are not able to see those flaws in your critic does not mean that your critic is a perfect specimen of human being. They simply hide their flaws well. This is why you need to remember that bad criticism simply does not affect you at all.

When facing a critic, it can be hard to react instantaneously. Sometimes, people plot their revenge to show their critics how awful they had been. However, revenge is not the solution to any problem. It just makes a small dispute much bigger. It makes you fret over something unnecessary. This all comes down to you remaining in the past and ignoring the present. That time can be better spent on other more

Teenagers copying to succeed?

productive things which would help you actually achieve something better in life. Here are a few ways that you can actually deal with criticism.

Carefree attitude

You need to either show your critics through your action that you are not what they were accusing you of, or you can simply turn the other way around and continue doing what you were already doing. Both of the conditions are meant to save you from worrying too much about something insignificant.

→ *sometimes badlying is not necessarily toward a real flaw*

When you are trying to show your critics that you can do something or eliminate a flaw that they pointed in you, you are actually working toward a better you. You are not just trying to show them that they are wrong, but you are doing something that may potentially help you make your life better. However, once you have shown them what you can do, you need to carry on what you are doing in order to benefit you completely. This will insure that you have not wasted your efforts on anything fruitless and will continue to make you a better person.

Chapter 3 is missing?

46

On the other hand, when you choose to accept that criticism without choosing to react, you are simply doing yourself a favor. Moreover, if you simply choose to forget what that person criticized you for, you are still way ahead in life. This is because when you chose not to overthink that critical analysis that someone did of you, you are simply investing the time in doing something productive. That productive thing could lead you to be more focused on the things that need your immediate attention. It could even be something as non-materialistic as love for the family. When you are not distracted by criticism, you are going to be more focused on the people whom you love and who love you back. You would be simply evaluating the positive things in life that you already have and in return you would be feeling good about your life.

OR thinking through knowing that it's not worth thinking.

Being Hateful

When you are criticized, even the humblest person can feel offended and angry at this unwanted criticism. This does not mean that everyone carries that hate around with them for a long time. Some simply let that hate go within a few minutes, while others work around it and try to get back to the person who criticized them. The usual response to someone who criticizes you is, "I hate this person. How dare he/she say that about me."

However, as mentioned earlier, this hate needs to end right there and then. Carrying it with you will only make you stuck to the past and not let you move forward. The more you think about how someone criticized you, the more it will bring your morale down. You would become self-critical and judge yourself too harshly. This is because in your hate toward the person who criticized you, you would be overanalyzing every little detail about yourself.

You may simply be angry at the fact that no one sees how good you are in other aspects of life. This anger can also evolve and slowly consume you, making you think that everyone who is there with you is always thinking about your flaws. Being paranoid is one of the many factors that can come when you hate your critics or yourself.

The more time you spend trying to find flaws in yourself, the more you will end up hating your life. This can simply lead you to be more depressed and will not let you be

find it, accept it & learn from it.

48

happy with you and your life. The best thing to do in a situation like this is to give up on hating and try to be a better person. When you become a person who is free of hate, you are simply going to feel much better and you will try to incorporate more positive things in your life rather than focus on anything negative.

Maintaining a Distance

When someone criticizes you, it is probable that they are doing it for your benefit. They may want to see you succeed in life which is why they want you to get better and point out the flaw that you can clearly improve on. However, one thing that you always need to maintain is the distance from the person who criticizes you only to demotivate you or make fun of you. A criticism can only be helpful if it is done to correct someone doing something wrong. If the criticism is only meant to downgrade the abilities of a person or simply make fun of them, then it is better to stay away from such criticism and the critic.

Maintaining a distance from people who like to point out your flaws is the best way to avoid any emotional battle

Removing yourself from toxic people

49

within yourself. Being exposed to a critic who continues to point out your flaws, without ever acknowledging your good point, is only going to bring you down one day or the other. It can make you hypersensitive to rejection and create a false sense of insecurity. The more insecure you are about yourself, the more approval you would yearn to get from others. When you are surrounded by a critic, you woult not get the encouragement you need and your condition would only get worse.

Going with the Flow

This going with the flow is not the one where you let your emotions get the best of you and let the journey of your life be full of surprises. Instead, it means that you simply let people talk about you and let them criticize you because you know you are completely immune to what they are saying to you.

However, this does not mean that you let people bad-mouth you. It does mean that when they point out a flaw, you simply laugh with them and accept that you have that flaw.

You then let them know that you are aware of anything bad that they are pointing out and this critic does not need to show you something that you are already aware of.

When these people realize that their attitude does not affect you, they are simply going to stop pointing out things and criticizing you. This may take time but it always happens. This is as simple as "If you can't beat them, then join them." and it is perhaps the best thing that you can do with your haters.

This trait is however especially present in those who have developed their emotional armor in a strong way. They know they cannot be harmed by other people's comments about their flaws. They have the ability to listen to criticism and still have a positive attitude toward their trait and toward the person criticizing them.

All of the points presented in this chapter add up to one simple thing that there are many ways to deal with criticism. However, all of these ways mean that you are going to have to be emotionally strong. Your emotional armor has to be designed in such a way that it protects you from any type of negative criticisms. On the other hand, it needs to be set up in a way that it lets you think about and act upon the criticism positively.

The more refined your armor is, the more it would work in your favor. Dealing with criticism in any of the above defined ways would simply mean that you are strong and capable of handling your emotions well.

No force will be able to infiltrate your emotional armor to affect you in any possible way. This is indeed the sole purpose of the emotional armor to prevent any obstacle from affecting the person emotionally and allow them to be strong.

Questions to Ask Yourself

Q. How to determine the intensity of the criticism you have been receiving?

Ans. It varies from person to person. At a workplace, if the criticism is from the boss, it is of high priority and you should try to work on it to prevent it in the near future. Similarly, criticism from a person in the neighborhood is of less importance and should not be considered intense at all.

↳ Disagree, criticism how manager does not necessarily has to righ dirat.

Q. What to do and not to do with criticism?

Ans. It depends on the nature of the criticism. It is not appropriate to get defensive or rude while receiving constructive criticism whereas it is suitable to ignore the criticism if the nature is destructive.

Q. Is it possible to utilize criticism?

Ans. Yes! Trying to learn from the criticism and improving yourself is the best way to deal with criticism. This is what the critic is least expecting from you.

not true if it was positive crinsian·

Chapter 4

Taking Constructive Feedback

As we have learned how to deal with criticism in the previous chapters and different impacts criticism can have on a person, this chapter will elaborate how an individual can determine whether the criticism by the opposing party is constructive or destructive for them. Imagine a person utilizing the constructive feedback they are receiving from others and using them for their self development and betterment. The drawback of mistaking constructive criticism with destructive criticism can cause disastrous results. This will also be discussed briefly.

Whenever there is progress, there will be criticism. Despite the nature of progress, the majority of people tend to push others down. It is actually quite rare to encounter constructive criticism these days as everyone is in

Source, don't agree.

competition with each other. Nobody wants others to get ahead of them. It is up to the individual how they decide to deal with the criticism and avoid taking any mental damage from it. Even though there have been many lessons on considering criticism as a positive factor and using it for your own progress, people do not tend to learn easily. We are now going to discuss destructive and constructive criticism one by one.

Destructive Criticism

There are two types of criticism that we may face in our lives. The most common one is the destructive criticism. The aim of people criticizing others is to drain the motivation of the individuals down and prevent them from progressing. There is no certain reason why people tend to *← their own insecurities* criticize others but it is safe to say that their criticism is interlinked with jealousy factor. It is often difficult for people to not feel jealous at all while seeing other people making progress in life. This usually occurs when critics tend to encounter competition in their specific field. It could be whether in studies, business, or any other field.

One of the problems that surface with most of the people is that they let critics break them down whenever critics want to instead of giving them a shut-up call for good. This should not be the case if they are planning on developing themselves.

Quite aggressive

There are several factors to be considered when a person is working on improving themselves. Out of these factors, one is to be persistent about your goals. This includes not letting critics break you down while you are climbing up the ladder of success. Critics tend to take every possible measure to degrade the person who is progressing even if they are not in competition with them. It is difficult at times to figure out why someone would opt to focus on your decline instead of working on themselves in becoming a better person. The hate from the critics can have immense effects on the victims, yet a strong person would not even bat an eye on whatever they are planning to do.

Constructive Criticism

The second form of criticism that a very few number of people are likely to have is constructive criticism which is the total opposite of destructive criticism. It can be easily judged by the name itself. This form of criticism is meant to encourage the person it is directed to so that they can become better. People who use this type of criticism are very rare as it tends to build the victim instead of breaking them down. This sort of criticism can be expected from family members, close friends, or anyone else who are concerned for your growth.

At first, to the victim, it seems as if there is no difference in constructive and destructive criticism but with a calm and thoughtful mind, it is easy to determine that constructive criticism from your beloved ones works as a source of motivation. As a matter of fact, even if constructive criticism tends to help the person in becoming a better person, some people never seem to understand it and rather take it as a negative hit against them. The victims should use constructive criticism in their favor.

There are a lot of people we can use as examples who used criticism in their favor despite the category in which it lies. Those people are now a great influence on the youth. People who are CEO of huge companies such as Bill Gates of Microsoft, Elon Musk of Space X and Tesla Incorporation, Mark Zuckerberg of Facebook, and Jack Ma of Alibaba are encouraging and motivating and urge people to stay dedicated to their desired field.

There are several other people who are featured in Forbes, some of them are also celebrities and artists. No matter what sort of family background they have, no matter how difficult or easy it was for them to deal with life, whether they had any support or not in becoming what they are, all of the personalities mentioned above give lessons on handling criticism.

There is no certain age when a person starts dealing with criticism but people tend to mistake life lessons as criticism. In this era, teenagers are rebellious toward their parents. [It is not farther from the truth that they wish to pursue in their life and achieve their goals in the long run but the approach seems absurd]

— what strategies; opinion & generalizing.

From an adult's perspective, the strategies opted by teenagers of this era are less professional than they should be. Instead of encouraging them to perform well, the parents simply let their children become on their own. We cannot deny the fact that our elders only seek ways that help us with developing ourselves but it is difficult for teenagers to understand this fact. Teenagers are using new ways for getting ahead in life, unlike our elders who used to believe that education will enable them to prosper in life. Our elders are not wrong but teenagers believe that education is not worthy at all as they read about the lives of influential people in the world.

— not necessarily; "elders" are not nece. Correct; emo to really abuse?

⤷ not really; different forms of education

We all agree that the majority of the billionaires or successful people were dropout from schools or colleges yet they were able to become successful with their intellectual skills and ideas of innovation. People influenced by such personalities tend to follow their footsteps and strategies to copy them instead of coming up with something on their own. Copying somebody else never leads to permanent success in life, this lesson by

↘ small % of ppl are dropouts

elders to the teenagers is considered as criticism which is totally irrelevant.

The factor mentioned above about criticism is the one faced by teenagers. On the other hand, people face real and severe criticism after entering adulthood when it comes to maintaining relationships with people around you. It is merely impossible to keep everyone happy and prevent them from criticizing or pointing fingers at you regardless of the fact whatever you are doing in life.

A wise man once said, "*If you want to make everyone happy, sell ice cream!*" which clarifies that it is not even possible to keep everyone happy at the same time if you want to prosper in your life and achieve something you have only dreamed of. A person should be strong enough to withstand destructive criticism at this stage of life in order to tackle other obstacles and critical situations in life, such as depression from devastating events, anxiety, and decline due to the financial crisis.

which
stage
life

depression
is a
sickness-

People should consider themselves lucky if they are encountering constructive criticism as it helps with building confidence and encourages them to be better. People are most likely to deal with it during their late teen years or early adulthood. It usually starts when teenagers get enrolled in high school and enter a whole different phase of life. The steps taken by their parents are to avoid the circumstances they have been through or might have seen other experiencing, yet it feels as if they are stopping them from living a normal life.

The constructive criticism gradually carries on with life as the individual enters different phases of life. It usually takes a person to reach the age of 20 years approximately to be aware of the fact that constructive criticism is in their favor. It can be utilized to avoid a lot of mistakes an individual is likely to make during their early adulthood.

To further elaborate the effect of constructive criticism on a person's life, I would like to paraphrase a story based on constructive criticism which will also highlight the consequences of destructive criticism in comparison. Born in the heart of United States of America, a child named Calvin was living along with one elder brother and one baby sister in addition to their parents in a normal household in Kansas.

Despite being a middle child, Calvin was a bright student since kindergarten and had always been outrunning other students in the class in the elementary school as well. All three of the children were beloved to their parents until Calvin's elder brother reached his early adulthood years. Just like the others, he also became a rebellious teen which resulted in arguments erupting between him and their parents. After not being able to cope up with his family, Calvin's elder brother decided to move out of the house and live on his own.

Their parents tried to stop him but they were unfortunate enough to lose him. Calvin was six years younger than him which made him easier to be under his brother's influence and follow his footsteps. Luckily, Calvin was on the right path and had been a responsible kid for his parents. After moving into high school, he entered a different phase of life which altered his personality.

This was a negative step in Calvin's life as his parents believed he was following steps of his elder brother. In order to prevent Calvin from being a rebellious teenager like his brother, his parents decided to look after him even more. They were taking extra measures to insure none of his desires remain unfulfilled, so he would not have to choose the wrong path.

Calvin thought that he was getting the special treatment due to the loss of his elder brother but he was unaware of the fact that the purpose of treating him special was to avoid having any negative thoughts in his mind. Despite the love and affection from his parents, things started to slightly tear apart between him and his parents similar to his brother's situation.

The reason behind such unrest was that Calvin wanted to pursue his career as a film producer while his family wanted him to be an engineer. The conflicts began when he asked his parents to enroll him in a film school to carry further his studies and passion for film-making.

Calvin's parents were not happy with his decision and started forcing him to opt for engineering. Unlike any other typical child, he threatened his parents that he would run away just like his brother if things did not go according to his will. This was the worst thing he could do to his parents as they were only concerned about his better future and wanted him to lead a better life.

Calvin somehow managed to convince his parents for film school and got enrolled before the first batch started, while his parents taunted that he would never be able to succeed without his parents' guidance. He was much dedicated toward the film school and determined to opt for film-making as his profession. His parents began to think that he might have made the right decision by enrolling himself in the film school as he was performing much better than he would perform while studying engineering.

Things started to settle between them and life was getting along smoothly until Calvin graduated from film school. He started to think that he soon would be making all of the decisions on his own and they would turn out to be in his favor. Little did he knew, his lack of experience in life was only going to cause him trouble.

Calvin's behavior was gradually changing back to being reluctant again. This time, all his parents wanted to do was correct his mistakes verbally instead of taking any action as he was mature enough to realize it. He started as an internee in a production house to brush up his skills and learn as much as he could. Meanwhile, he proposed the idea of financing a car from the bank to use it for his personal transportation. Being well aware of the terms and conditions of the bank and consequences of not being able to pay the installments, Calvin's father stated that it would be a big mistake at this stage to finance a car as his job was not permanent nor he had enough money saved to pay upfront.

Despite the advice from his father, Calvin opted to get a car financed by the bank on which his father said that he would not be able to afford such luxury at a young age. It seemed as if Calvin made the right choice until he was fired from his job after three months. He managed to pay installments for the car for another month after losing the job, but he was soon left with no money. He turned toward his parents and friends to ask for money and prevent the car from being taken away, but nobody helped him and he ended up losing the car to the bank.

Calvin blamed his parents for his slight decline in career as they criticized his decision. He also decided to move out instantly regardless of the fact that he had no place to go nor any money left for his survival. The furious decision he made was another step toward decline, but he soon managed to get hired by another production house which provided him mobile residence along with enough salary to fulfill his needs. Again, this decision felt like he did the right thing, but he was wrong once again.

Calvin believed he would work harder to settle down without taking help from anyone, but fate had other plans for him. He was approached by his parents who constantly tried to convince him to return home as they feared he would get himself involved in more trouble soon. Being a person with arrogant personality, he denied the offer and told them he would be fine on his own if they would leave him alone forever. His parents were devastated by his words but they had to be strong and make distant themselves from him. They told him that he was still an immature kid who would end up running back toward his family in the end.

Maybe they shouldn't have done that had been prepared

As per Calvin's parents, things started to fall apart again. Calvin had been saving a great sum of money to help him *[how do you know calvin (sour)]*

settle down once and for all. He had been planning a meeting with a mortgage company agent to get a house in his name. he decided to convert his savings into cash to pay a quarter of the price upfront to secure the home, but he got robbed three days prior to the meeting with the agent. This shook his soul and he had no idea what to do.

Devastated by the incident, Calvin was convinced to ask his organization for a loan to pay the mortgage on the house. Upon his request, he was told to stick to his mobile home until he is worthy enough to be granted a loan. He was triggered and furiously left the organization without having a second thought what he would do. With no other option left, he ended up returning home to his parents with tears of regret in his eyes. However, he was warmly welcomed back by his parents. Even though his father was furious toward him, a sight of Calvin melted his heart in a second. Calvin apologized for everything he had done to his family only for his greed to be successful in life while he ended up with gaining nothing but the experience of life.

Calvin was accepted by his family after some settlements and was looking forward to a new beginning of his life. He realized that the criticism he was facing previously could have been used in his favor as it was constructive criticism which he was mistaking for destructive criticism. He would have avoided losing the car in the first place if he would have listened to his father.

The robbery could have been avoided if Calvin had decided to return home when his parents requested him to. A lot of trouble could have been avoided if only he was wise enough to understand that all his parents wanted to do was for his betterment. However, he was starting his life again and was left with nothing but regrets. He was repeatedly being consoled by his parents to help him move. After the hustle bustle, he learned his lesson that *"it's better late than sorry."*

In order to determine if the other party is criticizing to build you up or break you down, the individual needs to have a clear and calm mind and think from a neutral perspective, favoring none of the sides in the process. Remembering how the relationships were between you and the parties can also be used to determine whether the group is speaking in your favor or against you. Several other ways can be used to determine the difference. Moreover, using constructive feedback will only help the person with becoming emotionally stronger than before.

The reason to paraphrase this story was to highlight the factor how mistaking constructive criticism for destructive criticism can lead to catastrophic aftermath in life. Various incidents can take place in the individual's life which can change the course of life. Learning to determine the difference between constructive and destructive criticism can save a person from falling into the pit of troublesome phases of life.

We are further going to discuss in the chapters how to handle insults and use them in your favor instead of letting them break you down. Building a long-lasting confidence is essential for everyone to help them prevent from taking a step back in life. Life is all about moving forward and dealing with people who are pointing fingers at you. This factor will also be covered in depth with examples to enable the readers to engage with the context of the book and understand the solutions to the problems that often arise.

Questions to Ask Yourself

Q. What to do if you are having trouble identifying the difference between '*Constructive*' and '*Destructive*' feedback?

Ans. Consult someone worthy of trust and seek help from them. It is better to have two different opinions on something instead of relying on only one perception.

Q. What to do if you are getting destructive feedback from your siblings? (if any)

Ans. It is recommended to have a brief discussion with you parents before any arguments take place within the family, as that may create an unhealthy environment for the entire family.

Q. How to avoid destructive feedback from having an impact on you?

Ans. If you receive destructive feedback from any individual despite their relationship with you, it is recommended to take the feedback lightly and not think about it again. Diverting your thoughts toward positive feedback will be of great help.

Chapter 5

Handling Insults

Now that we have cleared the concept of taking constructive feedback and letting it have an impact on your life, it is time to shed some light on the various types of insults and how you can handle them accordingly. Not letting insults have a bad influence on a person is actually a quality that is difficult to find in many individuals. Whether it is a swear word, a sarcastic comment, or a silly comeback during an argument, an individual should be emotionally strong enough to tackle it with ease.

A major problem that is prevalent in our society is that people are emotionally sensitive and allow other people to damage them internally regardless of the relationship with them. This happens even though most of the phrases that hurt people are not even swear words, they are just sarcasm as that seems to be a trend in the world today. People often

major problem that people are emotionally sensitive?

judge other people's intellectual skills based on their sarcastic comebacks or mocking statements about other people. It has become a part of human psychology to judge people's intellectual skills in such a manner. This is quite absurd actually, as there are several other factors, which can allow the person to determine the mentality and IQ level of the other person.

For the people who face trouble dealing with insulting comments and sarcastic statements, there are various methods to prevent the suffering. From not responding violently to avoiding about it, there are several ways to put in place an emotional armor and strengthen it with the passage of time. It would be appropriate to begin with the types of insults, their nature, and how they affect the person who is being insulted.

Criticism

The most common type of insult is criticizing. This may seem like a whole different thing, but it can actually make the victim feel insecure about their personality or whatever the other person is criticizing them about. There are two types of criticism: destructive and constructive criticism.

Both types of criticisms may seem harmful to some people. Suppose that there is an individual who is emotionally sensitive and cannot prevent an emotional breakdown; to such a person, both types of criticisms will be destructive. In order to avoid such situations, it should be essential for the individual to build a strong emotional armor and become less narcissist. If a person tends to maintain silence, others will try to break the emotional armor to manipulate their emotions without certain reasons, just like criticism. There is not always much interest that people have in others; they only critcize to play with other people's feelingsAn article by Lamiat Sabin in 2014 stated, *"teenagers tend to shut their brains down while being criticized."* As a matter of fact, teenagers face most of the criticism when their life is on the verge and they have to opt for a profession. Conflicts may erupt between the two generations living in the same household while coming to a conclusion regarding the teenager's profession. The teen may want to opt for something that is more viable from their perspective, but it may seem absurd to an adult based on their experiences in life.

[handwritten annotation: build: how?]

If the teen succeeds in convincing their parents to allow them to choose their desired profession, it will give birth to an infinite amount of criticism. This is more likely to have a negative effect on the mindset of the teenager, as they are not usually mature enough to deal with criticism constructively. Constant criticism of people of a certain age will only have a negative effect on personality of the young adult.

There is a possibility that it may not seem easy at first to become emotionally strong, but if a person is determined to change themselves, gradually everything will turn out to be in their favor. Life is all about being devoted to something that may seem difficult to achieve, but everything can be conquered with a firm belief. No matter how difficult it is or how long it might take you to overcome it, all of the efforts will be worth it in the end.

Taking a stand against the people who are willing to take you down and bury you in the ground will be the first step toward becoming emotionally strong. The second step will be to act arrogantly toward the people who can be labelled as '*haters.*' The last step will be to generate enough

bisagree.

confidence within yourself to not let such statements or comments affect you in any possible way.

Sarcasm

The second form of insult is sarcasm. This form of insult is quite fair for some people, yet there are some individuals who have trouble dealing with it. Sarcasm is usually used by young adults or teenagers in their friendly conversations and the reason behind it is to add humor to their comebacks during an argument. However, some sarcastic comebacks can be severe enough to hurt an individual's emotions without one's intentions to do so, while some may be mild enough to bear without any harm.

Some people may target other person's weakness in a sarcastic comeback in order to sound more brutal while it may cause emotional damage to the victim. Such insults should not be practiced amongst people as it is difficult to determine if the other person will be able to cope with the insult and take it lightly or if they would feel bullied and targeted.

Sarcasm seems like a fun thing but the damage it can do can be severe. Take this as an example, Kevin Hart (a famous stand-up comedian) is on a stage with over 5,000 people watching him doing stand-up comedy. He is cracking hilarious jokes, telling stuff about his life and passing sarcastic comments on the trending things. He calls up a volunteer from the crowd and decides to involve them in the act. If he chooses to use that person as a subject or a target for his jokes and sarcasm, the volunteer would not feel satisfied with his show anymore.

There are several chances of the volunteer feeling embarrassed in front of the crowd because of the sarcastic comments being told about them. It would still seem funny to the rest of the audience, but the volunteer might be regretting coming to the show in the first place. This may damage the individual internally and badly enough to make them suffer from a mental breakdown. Usually, people do not realize what impact they have on the victim until they can visibly see the consequences.

If the volunteer bursts in tears and cries out for being targeted, only then people would realize how big of a mistake it was. However, by the time people realize the mistake, it is usually too late. The moment of embarrassment has passed and now they are on the verge of a breakdown. All of this could be avoided if people start being more considerate toward what they utter and realize what effect it can have on the person. Lack of realization often leads to people becoming mentally ill and ending up being anti-social.

Swear Words

Using swear words is the last form of insult which has a clear concept of disrespecting the other individual, regardless of the nature of the argument or situation. Swear words are not meant to be used during a conversation or even a discussion as their sole purpose is to trigger the angry side of the other person which often results in a brawl. The usage of swear words is mostly frowned upon in social settings and it is not considered appropriate in most other situations. From a movie theatre to shopping center to schools and from offices to community halls, it is against the norms to use swear words. They are not only meant to trigger the bad side of the other individual, but they are also considered rude, as they tend to express meanings of rudeness and vulgarity toward the victim.

There seems to be no point of using swear words at all, but the modern generation tends to use swear words often to portray themselves as dominant or rebellious which is absurd actually. As a matter of fact, it often reveals how low the intellectual skills of a person are. There is nothing to be proud of in using swear words as they are only meant to degrade the other person in every context.

adults
use profanity
esp from (?)

People often use swear words to display their anger toward someone, but it never leads to anything except unrest between two people. It is impossible to think of a situation where using a swear word is considered appropriate. The main reason of every swear word is to offend and deliver the message of hate.

If a person is habitual of using swear words even when they do not want to, which is quite rare, then the person should learn to control their temper. If they are able to conquer their anger and temper, they will gradually overcome their habit of using swear words. This habit might be holding some people back in their life from establishing communication.

All the three types of insults and their impact will be further clarified in the following anecdote along with the strategy to overcome them. Moreover, these tips on becoming emotionally strong will help the readers to implement those strategies and change the course of their life.

Anecdote

The anecdote begins with the character named Bruce who was emotionally sensitive since he was a toddler. Born and raised in the suburban lifestyle, he did not have the chance to interact with other children. He belonged to a loving family of five members which consisted of Bruce living with his parents alongside his elder brother and sister. Bruce was the youngest, yet not the most adored. His parents loved all three of them equally. After completing his high school, Bruce was soon to be enrolled in a university which was out of the city. Unlike his siblings, he was convinced to get enrolled in a college far from his hometown.

It was no secret that he was an introvert and never had the guts to speak up against anything, yet he had to move away. Regardless of the fact that he was going to have trouble meeting new people and establishing communication with them, Bruce took the bus to the neighboring city, which was 400 miles south from his hometown. It was a long journey but he managed to sleep during it. Upon arriving, he was somehow confident that he would settle down in the new city in a couple of days, but the odds were not in his favor.

One week prior to his joining the college, he witnessed the most annoying neighbors one could have. They were the type of neighbors who undervalued him and did not care at all if they were rude to him.

As Bruce was an introvert, he decided to adjust to those people instead of responding to their rude behavior and absurd acts which would most likely give birth to pointless arguments as per his perception of them. The more he tried to ignore his annoying neighbors, the more they would undervalue him and taunt him for being arrogant as he never used to talk much with anyone in his surroundings.

Their reluctant behavior was getting on Bruce's nerves, but he was too much reticentto break the ice and call them out for their rudeness. He did not know that he was capable of giving a shut-up call to his neighbors; all he needed was a spark to take a stand.

Bruce joined his college and began socializing with his fellows, but he could not give up his habit of plucking himself out of a group every once in a while to feel distant from everybody on purpose. His friends assumed he was homesick, while he was just having trouble with the neighbors and their pointless criticism. He was too shy to break the silence and explain the scenario to his friends.

Adopting to the situation seemed fair enough to him and he acted upon it as well. He soon made a friend who was relatively close to him as compared to the rest of the group. His friend became the reason to change Bruce's personality; however, unintentionally, his friends got comfortable enough with him to use sarcastic comments in order to add a little humor in every conversation.

The level of sarcasm was moderate enough to cope up with at first, but it soon became unbearable for Bruce as they started joking about his family conditions and how he had come out of a suburban household.

Bruce felt devastated for being centrally targeted and started acting strangely. His insecurities were causing mental sickness to him, but he was strong enough to fight them back. His transition in behavior was quite noticeable to his friend and he was determined to figure out the reason behind it. Upon insistence, Bruce opened up about his trouble with the neighbors and harsh sarcasm from his friends.

Bruce's friend felt miserable for him and wanted to help. Despite being a close friend, he could do nothing except offering him verbal support. He assured Bruce that he was going to help him in every possible way and he became his listener; a person who would listen to his daily struggles and the stories from his childhood. He started telling him how his childhood was different from the rest of the kids for never having friends.

The first semester was over and it was time to pay the fee. Bruce contacted his parents to ask for the fee and they transferred it immediately, but with a message. The message stated that they might not be able to afford the fee next semester, therefore he should look for a source of income as they do not want him to discontinue his studies either. They added that they would try as much as they can to support him throughout his journey.

This worked as a source of motivation for Bruce and he started looking for hourly-based jobs. He was fortunate enough to get hired as a cash register operator at a retail store with a relatively better wage than his friend. Everything was fair in his life until he exchanged pleasantries with his boss at work. Bruce could not believe his ears when he realized that despite being a successful entrepreneur, his linguistic skills consisted of swear words.

This was a huge setback for Bruce as he was facing all three forms of insults at once. It was time for him to buckle up and take control of the events occurring in life. His friend suggested him to consult a psychiatrist. Upon meeting, the psychiatrist observed Bruce and inquired about the incidents that were disturbing him. After the session was over, Bruce decided to opt for a course with a psychiatrist in order to change his personality and live his life based on principles of an emotionally strong person.

This was a great initiative by him and his friend, and a clear change in Bruce's personality was visible. Weeks passed and Bruce was keeping up with the course of his psychiatrist. He was disciplined enough to tackle the criticism of his neighbors.

Bruce got a job after college which allowed him to stay away from the house most of the time. For the rest of the day, he would indulge himself in activities that kept his mind away from people who could cause trouble to him. This was the sign of progress toward a new start for him and a big change in his personality occured. Soon enough, he started to develop his sense of humor which allowed him to respond to sarcastic comebacks intellectually without being offended at all. This transition was appreciated by his friend. Bruce started to blend in with the rest of the group.

In a matter of two months, Bruce was able to overcome two of the main types of insults he was insecure with.

Bruce could not believe the change he was seeing in himself. From an introvert to an ambivert leading toward being an extrovert, he never expected this would happen. With the passage of time, he was able to switch his workplace as well which also enabled to get over the third form of insult. The things that were once keeping him from socializing and being under peer pressure now became his strongest traits.

He was able to lead a much better life than he ever did before. He could not thank his friend enough for being his supporter during the journey of transition of his personality. He believed it would not have been possible if his friend was not determined to bring the light of positivity in his life.

The anecdote is the perfect example how the determination of an individual can change their entire course of life. Despite how crucial the phase is or how reluctant the people are around them, there is nothing that can stop a person from changing themselves into a better person. All it takes is a firm belief and one step forward; in time, you will lead your life according to your will, not by the way others want you to.

We are further going to elaborate how to build a lasting confidence which will lead us to the conclusion of the book which is of finally displaying your armor after taking all of the aspects into consideration briefly and building a better personality than before.

Questions to Ask Yourself

Q. What to do if you're having trouble dealing with one of your friends' sarcastic behavior?

Ans. Confront them immediately and make them aware of their unpleasant behavior which can become the root cause of conflict between you and your friend. It is never beneficial to lose a friend.

Q. How to respond to insults from people with less importance in your life?

✓ But if you're copying mechanism is to respond

Ans. It would be wise to stay quiet and not respond to them at all rather than trying to outsmart them by responding and ending up looking like a fool. The phrase *"The best answer to a fool is silence"* suits the context of this answer.

Q. Is it advisable to develop the habit of sarcastically insulting others?

Ans. A big NO! If you tend to develop the habit of sarcastically insulting someone, you are already pushing them away from you. Nobody prefers being in contact with someone who has the intentions of insulting others.

Q. How to control aggressive response to swear words and insults.

Ans. For the people with short temper or the tendency to react aggressively to something said against them or a statement that might upset them, it is advisable to engage themselves in activities that can help ease their anger and aggressiveness.

Q. Is crying an option?

Ans. It may seem like a very rare question, but people often end up crying after being insulted or humiliated in front of a number of people. It allows them to feel better and get over the incident relatively faster, so it is alright to cry no matter what your gender is.

Chapter 6

Building a Long-lasting Confidence

As we've covered several factors in the previous chapters such as dealing with criticism, taking positive criticism and being able to determine the difference between constructive and destructive criticism along with how to deal with insults and what they can do to a person with weak or almost no emotional armor, it's time to focus on the last factor which is building long-lasting confidence.

Now, many of us may know that confidence is the key to success. It helps people succeed in many aspects throughout different age groups. For instance, if a student from high school is determined to enter the world of entertainment and become an actor, he or she needs confidence. If this student participates in a theater act or any other relevant activity which involves acting in front of even a small number of crowdwithout the confidence needed to do so, he/she is most likely to fail. If they aren't able to gather up enough confidence to act or perform in front of a minor crowd in school, how will they be able to act in front of a whole production team which is recording the acting scenes which, later on, will be included in the movie which will be shown worldwide? The point here is clear: if the foundation of your confidence is weak, it's going to be quite difficult to tackle obstacles in life in the long run.

Confidence is not only limited to acting or singing at "*X Factor*", it is essential in every situation you will meet in the world. There are going to be several examples stated below to make it easy to determine why it is necessary to have confidence in yourself.

Consider that there's a person who was born and brought up in a middle-class household like the majority of the people and had to go through several hardships and incidents in life involving the death of his loved ones. After a decade, the person ended up being one of the most influential personalities on the planet and is featured in

'*Forbes*' and '*TedEx*'. He wants to talk about all his struggles to survive and his dedication towards something that made him a man he is now. He wants to tell people to show them that there's hope for everyone and there's nothing wrong in being different; he wants to let them know that nothing can stop them from achieving what they want to be. Now, how would it be possible to portray his message through interviews and motivational talks if that individual lacks confidence?

If a person is required to have an immense amount of confidence, it doesn't necessarily mean that they are destined to be a singer or an actor. Speaking your heart out and opening up yourself to the world to show them what made you strong actually requires confidence. *A bit contradictory to the book*

A little while ago, Sky Academy conducted a survey with 1,600 youngsters to determine how confident they are in life. The aim of the survey campaign was to boost the low self-esteem of the people selected for the survey. Among those 1,600 people, 60% of the girls claimed that they were confident, while the percentage of boys was 67% who were confident.

The rest 37% of the youngsters ranging from 14 to 17 year old stated that they felt more confident on social media platforms rather than in person. The social media was accused of draining the self-esteem among the youngsters despite the advantages people have these days because of it. Back to the survey, even though girls were able to out-perform boys in the 2015 GCSE Academic results by almost 8.4%, scoring grades ranging from A* to C, boys still outnumbered girls in being confident with the percentage of 67%, while girls remained at 60% only.

When the girls were interviewed and asked why they didn't feel confident, almost two-thirds of the girls said that it was because they felt insecure about their looks. In the pursuit of looking more attractive than other girls, their self-esteem was drained and they started to lose confidence. Out of the rest of the girls interviewed, one stated that they felt quite confident while interacting on social media, but a major factor is cyberbullying or ransomware which targets girls generally.

This not only drains their self-esteem and confidence, the threats also have a negative impact on their life and may result in a long-lasting negative effects on their brain. Even though parents play an essential role in supporting their child and boosting up their confidence, some cases are critical in which parents have very little influence on their child's life. The same survey also revealed that the majority of the parents and young people aged between 11 and 24 have a firm belief that confidence or self-esteem is an important factor in life.

Talking about confidence, I would like to state one of the problems that I faced while I was young and had low self-esteem. Gradually overcoming that problem of confidence allowed me to become a person better than before which also made me less dependent on others. I remember when I got my first job and had started actually earning money; that was when I felt that it was time to become more practical.

It was my job's requirement to have a bank account, so it would be easy to transfer the salary every month. So far, living the life of an introvert was slightly difficult as I wasn't socializing with people much, but now the course of my life was changing. I was always concerned about my appearance and my impression on the opposite person which disabled me from gathering up the confidence to talk to someone regarding any concerns whether personal or not.

I hated my existence and believed that I was worthless only because I lacked confidence in performing the everyday tasks of life. This time, however, I finally decided to change myself. When I visited the bank, I regretted my decision immediately as I could see a huge number of people inside the building and it made me insecure.

I wanted to go back outside and head home instead of getting on with the process, but it would have been one of the biggest mistakes of my life. I finally managed to head up to the universal teller counter and inquired about my concern. It nearly took an hour for me to get everything done before I could finally return home and not feel insecure about myself anymore.

Upon returning, I felt the vibes of accomplishment. For many people out there, it may seem like an ordinary task to walk inside a bank and perform their desired task, but it wasn't easy for me at all. Accomplishing this task became a

Stepping outside your comfort zone to make long lasting lifechanges.

step forward towards boosting my self-esteem and confidence.

There was a time when visiting the bank seemed like a difficult task to me and gradually I became one of the most social people in my family. All of this was because I was able to figure out why I was lacking confidence and I understood what could be done to overcome it.

The steps which I took to overcome the problem was to determine what was damaging my confidence in the first place; without knowing the root cause, it would be impossible to eradicate the problem which is the initial step. The second step which I believed was essential was to avoid negative self-talk. I see many people talking to themselves in a negative manner which is not healthy for the mindset and their emotional armor. Preventing such an act should be prioritized. The third step I intended to follow was to connect with the people who I believed were close to me.

Being surrounded by or communicating with people who adore you, admire you or even appreciate your presence is another step ahead in changing your perception of life.

Their positivity and love towards you will convince you into believing that the negative self-talk you've been doing lately was useless and you're not worthless at all. Your presence matters to them and you have a place in their life. The fourth step is to portray a confident personality. I believe it is not an easy task at all, but it is not impossible either. The determination to change yourself will ease the task and the goal will be achieved with the passage of time.

Everybody faces difficulties in portraying a confident personality, but the individual should have a firm belief to make it possible. The fifth step towards increasing your self-esteem is challenging yourself or setting a goal. If you aim to achieve something and start working on it, the likelihood of you succeeding in something you love increases dramatically.

Breaking a big task informally into small tasks.

The sixth step is to focus on your abilities and positive side. After you've done eradicating the negative thoughts from your life, it is time to focus on the positive aspects of your life to improve your self-esteem and increase your confidence. The last step towards becoming a confident person is taking care of yourself. When you find yourself progressing towards the goal of being confident, you should take care of yourself and avoid letting any criticism or insult break your barrier.

It will take time to build up enough confidence to tackle criticism and insult with ease, but the dedication and struggle will be worth it. It will allow you to lead a better and happier life as nothing will be strong enough to affect you in any way. Furthermore, you will be able to mentor others and help them out in getting out of the phase and improving their lifestyle as well.

As we've discussed earlier, confidence will not only allow the person to pursue their dream of being an actor or singer or a motivational speaker, but it will help them in almost every aspect of their life. If a person has a weak emotional armor and every criticism towards them turns out to be destructive even if it was constructive and every insult affects them, they will suffer from many problems throughout their life if they are not determined to change themselves.

Once they decide to change themselves and succeed in achieving their goal, nothing will be able to stop them from doing whatever they wish to do. Attacks of criticism and insults will have no power over them anymore. The person will be mature enough to deal with such things more effectively and efficiently throughout their life.

It is true to some extent that as the person grows old, the problems tend to become harder as well. As the problems in life get more difficult, the person also matures with time and their emotional armor becomes stronger. The person doesn't have to go through the difficult phase all over again to cope with the new challenges in life, he would be already strong enough to improvise and struggle his way through tough times.

he or she?

Yes, family, friends and other loved ones will act as support and will play major roles in your life, but there will be some problems which will remain hidden from them and you will have to face them alone. Recall the character from the anecdote mentioned in the previous chapter where the introverted person who was born and raised in a suburban area and never had friends was convinced to move away from his hometown to continue his studies at a higher level.

He faced all three types of insults (as mentioned in chapter 5 "handling insults") while trying to fit in the new environment.

There were times when he regretted moving away from his family in the first place and he wanted to run away, but his friend played an essential part in turning his life around as he was determined to help him and make him a better person. The character seemed to become an ideal person who was emotionally strong enough to tackle every obstacle in life and he was glad that he had made the decision to stay and seek his friend's help. His story is a clear and fine example of how a person can change with the passage of time and how much effect their emotional armor can be in changing their personality.

There might be a lot of people out there similar to the one mentioned in the anecdote who will be facing insults and letting them break their confidence down or some people might be having determining the difference between constructive and destructive criticism, both will feel like destructive criticism to them which will have definitely have a negative impact on their personality. Above all, there may be someone facing all of the factors mentioned above and they might end up suffering from mental illness such as anxiety, depression or insecurity. In order to prevent that from happening, we're going to pose a few questions and give solutions to the problems faced by people which will help the readers in identifying their problems and finding solutions to it.

Being confident allows people to stand out in public in a unique manner and they will be identified by their unique characteristics. Confidence will allow you to walk with the right attitude wherever you go instead of feeling shy or insecure about anything. This is relatively important as everyone believes that *"first impression matters"*.

The idea behind this phrase is that when you meet a new person, they can easily determine and judge your personality by the way you present yourself to them and carry the conversation ahead. It is the case with almost everyone. Being confident will also allow you to maintain eye contact with people while having a conversation. Not being able to maintain eye contact is a sign of low confidence and self-esteem and it also puts an impression that the person is ill-mannered. A person should have the guts to maintain eye contact thoroughly while having a conversation to show that they are confident about what they are saying.

> About being confident in your own skin.

Having confidence will also change your appearance as confident people are more concerned about their looks and overall fitness. Being physically attractive will allow you to engage in more conversations with people which requires → relative confidence. Furthermore, being physically attractive will give a positive impression to the people you will meet for the first time in your life. Another sign of being confident is having firm belief in yourself and your decisions. Not deviating from your opinions and decisions and having firm belief in them will allow the people around you to ← Believe but be open to determine that you're confident towards everything you say new ideas or do. People that lack confidence will not be able to do so. & concepts.

The tone of your voice also determines how confident you are while talking to someone. Having a low and mild tone may seem to be polite, but there is a chance that the person isn't confident and they can be put under pressure if the opposite person has a dominant personality which is a drawback for the person. As we towards the final characteristic of identifying a confident person, the second last one is standing up for others.

If a person has a strong tone, an attractive appearance and every other factor, it's time for them to help others. If you see a person being bullied or suffering from anxiety or depression, you should play your role and stand up for them. If they are being suppressed, you should be capable of helping them out in every possible way despite your relationship with them. It can be considered as an act of serving humanity which is a good deed; a little act of kindness will pay back soon in a much better way. You never know when you will need help and at the time that you do need it, your good deeds done in the past will help come back to reward you and ease your difficulty.

The last characteristic is doing what is rightful which is similar to the previous characteristic. It is not easy to do what is right as you may have insecurities that someone might get offended or show anger towards you and you might end up dealing with criticism or insults. However, being confident will allow you to do the right things

Give up no expectations of receiving

without hesitation. The rightful act may include sacrificing your '*want*' for someone's '*need*'. It is more likely to give you the vibe of satisfaction if you do what's right even if it feels difficult at first.

Keeping all the factors mentioned above in mind, I would like to conclude this chapter and state that, similar to other chapters, this chapter elaborately discussed its own problems to their root cause and also provided solutions. So far, the book has covered major aspects that needed to be discussed in order to allow a person to develop their emotional armor and ensure that it is strong enough to withstand any form of criticism (constructive or destructive) or insult. Below mentioned will be some of the tips and answers to the questions that may arise in the reader's mind to further clarify any misconceptions.

Questions to Ask Yourself

Q. What to do if you have trouble in class participation?

Ans. Try to pay more attention towards the questions being asked in the class and reduce the fear of being criticized as everyone shares their opinions inside the classroom.

Q. What benefit is a person with lasting confidence likely to have?

Ans. The person is more likely to lead a better life than before and will be able to perform several tasks with ease. It includes mainstream tasks such as communicating with new people and some major tasks such as participating in a presentation during a business meeting.

Q. Is it harmful to have confidence at any certain point?

Ans. Confidence is harmless for an individual unless they get overconfident and speak without care about something not taking into account the environment or surroundings.

Overconfidence

Q. What if a person has no one to support them?

Ans. Everyone will have at least one friend or acquaintance who are going to work as a support system for them throughout various phases of their life. If not, they will surely find someone who will understand and help them in changing the course of their life.

Online/support Groups
community

Q. Where to find the motivation to change yourself and become confident?

Ans. Listening to motivational speakers will help in boosting up your self-esteem and thinking out of the box. You are more likely to generate the urge to become more confident in life.

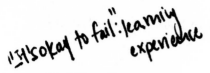
"It's okay to fail": learning experience

Q. What if you fail?

Ans. Its never too late to start all over again for the sake of success. As a matter of fact, a peron never fails. Either they succeed in the journey or they learn from the experience and avoid repeating those mistakes again.

Chapter 7

Displaying Your Emotional Armor

As we progress towards the conclusion of the book, the final chapter will cover all of the aspects to ensure that the readers have understood the concepts and the main objective of the book have been completed. So far, we've covered aspects such as: the foundations of building an emotional armor, the advantages of having an emotional armor, dealing with criticism, determining the difference between destructive and constructive criticism and utilizing constructive criticism in building and developing yourself up.

We further discussed handling insults and the last factor was developing a lasting confidence along with their benefits. This chapter is going to summarize all of the factors mentioned above along with an anecdote which will lead the readers towards the conclusion of the book followed by some of the benefits which will allow the readers to clarify their concept of displaying their strongly developed emotional armor. Below stated are the summaries of the chapters in chronological order as a rewind of the entire book.

In the first chapter, we raised questions to determine how many people have actually been through emotional problems, how many people find it difficult to face emotional attacks from other people despite their relationship with them. That chapter was dedicated to urging the readers to identify their problems and finding solutions to them. Without identifying the problems you're facing, it will be difficult to find a solution for them in the first place and you're more likely to keep experiencing the problems over and over again.

As we moved on to the next chapter, we discussed the fundamentals of building an emotional armor as it was necessary to ensure that the readers are well aware of the fundamentals in order to build an armor for themselves and further strengthen it as they progressed. Building an emotional armor was stated as being essential to prevent yourself from taking emotional damage as it can cause a tremendous amount of mental and emotional illness to the victim. This chapter worked as a guide for the readers in understanding the basics of emotional armor.

In the third chapter, the aim of the author was to guide the readers on how to deal with criticism. Criticism can either help you in developing yourself or destroy your personality. *Developing your Emotional Armor* will play an essential role in enabling the readers to avoid maximum damage caused by criticism. They will learn how they can actually use their emotional armor to build themselves up. Criticism was further divided into two different types which were elaborated on in the next chapter with an example story to further clarify the concept of criticism and how to differentiate between the types. It was also discussed how to use positive criticism in your self-development.

Derived from the third chapter, our fourth chapter was focused on taking constructive feedback. The aim of this chapter was to guide the readers in determining the differences between constructive and destructive feedbacks. Not being able to determine the difference can lead to mistaking constructive feedback as destructive feedback which will only result in having a negative impact on the victim. If a person is able to utilize constructive criticism/feedback, they are more likely to correct their mistakes and not give a reason or leeway to others to criticize them. It was also stated that it can be difficult for an individual at first to determine the basic differences, but it can surely help them in growing better than before.

Our fifth chapter was focused on handling insults. Three types of insults were elaborated in the chapter along with their solutions. An anecdote was also incorporated which was paraphrased in the chapter. It was done to ensure that readers would clearly understand all three types of insults and understand the measures that can be taken to prevent any negative effect of the insults. Even though sarcasm seems like fair play, in truth it works as a slow poison and can harm the relationship between two individuals. The character in the anecdote experienced all three of them which caused him several hardships. The belief of his friend to change him emotionally and develop an emotional armor led the character towards being a strong person who could tackle many obstacles in life and not let any type of insult affect them or get to them.

As we progressed gradually towards the conclusion of the book, we went through the sixth chapter which was dedicated to building lasting confidence. The reason why we need confidence was briefly discussed from various aspects of life and it was further stated how the person can build confidence.

A personal experience was also paraphrased in order to make the readers feel comfortable about themselves and to learn that lack of confidence can be found in anybody. They were also informed that confidence is actually required to complete everyday tasks such as engaging in a conversation with a new person or giving a motivational speech about your life in front of a number of people.

This chapter has summarized the book and is now going to paraphrase a story which will include the main factors and aspects of the book and ensure that readers understand

no development of main character

every concept of the book. Incorporated below will be the story of our main character who will tackle a few obstacles in his life followed by a traumatic incident and a roller coaster of emotions till they end up developing a strong emotional armor which changes the course of their life.

The story begins with the character named '*Jones*' who was born and raised in New York City. The hustle bustle of the people on the streets and the daily traffic jam was the environment in which Jones was brought up.His parents were well off and the environment around Jones never allowed him to suffer from isolation which seemed like a good thing at first. However, the challenges of life demanded a much emotionally stronger Jones. A series of difficult and dark phases of life awaited Jones before he could taste success.

Unlike other children, Jones was different. He envied various artists ever since he was in elementary school. Despite not being able to draw well at an early age, he was able to name various artists just by looking at their artwork. Jones was a talented child and had always been in the good books of his teachers. Even though art was his favorite subject, he was always able to outperform other students from elementary to high school.

Jones's parents were concerned about his future since he was their only child, but he was too young during the elementary years to learn things other than were taught at school. Jones' parents decided to wait till he was enrolled in High School to convince him and allow him to pursue his passion for being an artist. During the elementary years, Jones' gained great knowledge regarding his passion. With the passage of time, his interest was developing at a great rate. Soon after Jones got enrolled in high school, he was gifted his first set of paint brushes with canvas to put his passion into action. Regardless of being new to the canvas, Jones was able to paint the canvas as if he were a student of college who had been practicing art for a long time.

Without wasting further time, his parents decided to enroll him in an *"Art School"* to enable him to learn how to paint from scratch and then to move on to the advanced level. After joining the art school, Jones' parents received a call from the principal of the art school, requesting them to meet the teacher and the principal on a short notice. They got worried if Jones' might have been involved in an incident at the art school. Upon reaching and inquiring about why they were asked for a meeting on such a short notice, they were welcomed warmly and asked about Jones' passion for art. The authorities of the art school appreciated Jones' dedication and love for art; his parents were told that Jones' was already outperforming other students in his class despite being enrolled for 2 weeks only.

The meeting was long and full of compliments for Jones' ability which convinced his parents to take him out for dinner at a place of his choice. Jones was satisfied with his progress in the art school and was determined to keep up his firm in order to become one of the best painters of his school. Everything for Jones was going smoothly until he decided to ask out a girl named Lisa for the prom night in High School. Jones had liked that girl for a long time, but couldn't gather enough confidence to initiate a conversation with her at all. After his friends kept pushing him towards her for over a week prior to the prom night, he ended up asking her for the dance to which she responded positively. It was a chance for Jones to have conversations on daily basis with her.

Jones gathered up as much confidence as he could to start conversations with her. Fortunately, he was successful and they became great friends prior to the prom night. Without thinking twice, Jones expressed his feelings towards Lisa and asked her out. (The proposal) resulted in an immediate rejection which was a huge setback for Jones at that time. He was devastated by the rejection and couldn't figure out what went wrong. He had thought of Lisa as the perfect girl for over a year before he finally gathered up the confidence to ask her out. The rejection further drowned all of the confidence Jones had gathered up and he was now experiencing isolation. Jones' depression was clearly visible to his parents and they offered him as much emotional help as they could in order to pull him out of the dark phase of his life. *Understanding why*

Jones' parents decided to take him for a trip to France to inspire him so that he would continue to pursue his passion of being an artist. It took several weeks for Jones to get back on track and get over the setback he had experienced previously. He was regretting his decision of going to the prom with Lisa and even asking her out. Without realizing it, however, Jones had only gained experience from the setback and he was getting stronger than before. Months after getting back on track and practicing painting again, he was able to participate in an art competition held in California. Jones had to travel all the way from New York City to California for the sake of the competition in which he ended up securing the first position among many other competitors from different cities. This enhanced Jones' confidence and his parents were delighted to see the change.

Soon after the competition, Jones graduated from high school to college, but he was fortunate enough to stay in New York as the college was located within the city. Jones' parents decided to gift him a brand new car as a gift for graduating from high school. After purchasing the car, his parents decided to drive the car home all the way from Spring Valley back to New York City. While on their way back, his parents were involved in a tragic accident on the freeway in the middle of the night. The rescue vehicle reached to the site after an hour of the accident as there was no one to report it. Luckily, they were able to survive the accident, but Jones' father was admitted to hospital as his condition was quite critical. Several days after the accident, Jones lost his father.

This traumatic incident shattered Jones. Due to his father's death, his support system was torn apart. Jones' life was now missing a huge chunk which had played the essential part in bringing him back on track from disappointing or devastating events in his life. His mother alone could not manage everything as she was also facing a hard time in getting stable again. The void could not be filled for at least a year until Jones' mother decided to marry another man. Jones was never in favor of his mother's decision which resulted in him eventually leaving his house for good with whatever he had in his name. A happy, loving family had broken down in a time span of only one year. Jones had to face brutal and destructive criticism from people around him for his decision to live elsewhere.

Jones' emotional balance was getting unstable every day due to the struggle he was going through lately. He opted to meditate for a couple of weeks to seek inner peace and find solutions to the hardships he was facing. With the help of a mentor in seeking peace, he realized he should learn how to identify constructive feedback/criticism and utilize it for his betterment. Jones was quite confident that he will be able to improvise his emotional balance and things will turn out in his favor. It took a great deal of effort for Jones to regain his confidence and enhance his skills in determining the difference between constructive and destructive criticism. By the time he was done practicing meditation, Jones was capable of utilizing constructive criticism in his favor. He was developing his emotional armor gradually with immense strength.

Jones continued with his practice of painting till he graduated from college and opted for art as his profession. Right after graduating from college, Jones was approached by Lisa; she wanted to apologize and make up for whatever unease was between them due to her rejection of him. Her charming appearance and the vibes from the past were enough to make Jones' knees wobble and melt his heart, but he was emotionally strong enough to forgive her and move on without letting her enter his life ever again. This was the greatest progress so far for Jones in terms of being emotionally strong as he didn't have to worry about controlling his feelings anymore.

As Jones entered the practical world, it was time to portray his positive image and put his mark in the universe. His career started with a bump when few competitors insulted him sarcastically as he was the youngest of them all. Some even ended up using swear words to degrade him and stop him from progressing, because they were able to sense that Jones was going to give them a good run for their money.

Jones responded maturely to the criticizers and people defaming him instead of letting them break him down. He had finally developed a strong emotional armor and he was invincible against emotional attacks. Jones was now displaying his emotional armor to the world. He was not letting criticism or insult affect him in any way and penetrate his emotional armor. He was ready to deal with the world without letting down his guard.

Jones never had an idea that he would go through an entire roller coaster of emotions, ending up being so strong that he would be living independently by the age of 21. After displaying his emotional armor to the world and not letting anything affect him, he was ready to take on big challenges in life and pursue his dreams of being a great artist. After a few years of struggle, he became a renowned artist with a net worth of several million dollars; his conditions were even better than all that his father had been able to provide to their family when he was alive. It was all because Jones decided to build himself strong enough to tackle the hurdles in his life.

The story incorporated above was aimed at covering all the major aspects of the book in a summarized manner to clarify to the readers that emotional attacks can come from anywhere at any time, even from the people you least expect them from. The struggle of Jones' life was a great example of how difficult a few phases of life can be; it also told readers that the determination to be strong can lead one to becoming the fittest amongst everyone around them.

Displaying your emotional armor was generalized in the story incorporated, but it can be displayed in various phases of life. For instance, if there's a kid being bullied at school, his strong emotional armor can work as a shield for him, if displayed. Similarly, women can use their emotional armor to stand against harassment of any sort.

Developing and finally displaying your emotional armor will be the biggest initiative of your life as it will change the whole perspective of your life. A person may be in a decline and suffering from emotional breakdowns due to the emotional attacks from people around him including the people he believed that acted as his support system. A strong emotional armor will prevent such emotional breakdowns and the words of criticism and insult will no longer affect the individual in any way. In the worst case scenario, it will decrease the effect of emotional damage and a person would no longer have to go through the same emotional breakdown over and over again.

With the hope that this book has been a helpful guide for readers, I would state that I believe we all can develop a strong emotional armor to tackle with emotional attacks which tend to break us down. Using your emotional armor at the right time may result in making you emotionally invincible.

Below mentioned will be the conclusion of the book which review the benefits of displaying emotional armor; this has been included for the people who might have any misconception regarding the book. Following the conclusion will be several questions along with theirs answers that may arise in the minds of the readers to further understand the book.

The result of finally displaying your emotional armor will be much better than a person can ever expect. We will be avoiding the negative energy around us and also the people who are not good for our mental health. We will be escaping from the loop of emotional attacks causing damage to our mindset and perception. We will be fighting against the people standing against us by staying calm and not responding violently. Not suffering from an emotional breakdown anymore will also be a major benefit of displaying your emotional armor.

We will be disengaging and disconnecting from the people who are a bad influence on us. They can be anyone around us and we will be able to disconnect from them if they are a negative impact on our lives. Furthermore, we will not only lead a better life, but we will also forget the dark past we may have encountered. Forgetting the past is always going to be the initial step towards leading a happy and satisfied life, free from the worry of the past haunting us.

→ the past can't be forgotten, only coped & learnt from.

→ History in general reminds us not to forget the past but to embrace it & learn from it.

Questions to Ask Yourself

Q. What is essential before displaying emotional armor?

Ans. Identifying the strenths and weaknesses of your armor
to ensure that it remains indestructible at all times.

**Q. Are there any effects of emotional armor on the
family?**

Ans. As long as the individual knows when and where to
display his/her armor, there will be no such negative effects
on the family or the loved ones.

What about being closed off?
didn't mention about the balance

**Q. What if the armor is not capable to withstand
insults?**

Ans. It indicates that the armor lacks strength and needs to
be improved and updated.

Made in the USA
San Bernardino, CA
10 April 2018